Mary Boleyn
in a Nutshell

Copyright © 2015
MadeGlobal Publishing

ISBN-13: 978-84-943721-1-7

M
MadeGlobal Publishing

For more information on
MadeGlobal Publishing, visit our website:
www.madeglobal.com

For Mum
xx

Contents

Introduction

But if I were at my liberty and might choose, I ensure you, master secretary, for my little time, I have tried too much honestly to be in him, that I had rather beg my bread with him than to be the greatest queen in Christendom. And I believe verily he is in the same case with me; for I believe verily he would not forsake me to be a king.

– Mary Boleyn writing to Thomas Cromwell about her second husband William Stafford.

Who was Mary Boleyn? When this question is posed to people a variety of answers include "Anne Boleyn's sister", "Henry VIII's mistress", "Mother of Henry VIII's children", "That girl played by Scarlett Johansson in that movie…", "a mystery woman" and "a woman used by her family and then discarded". She was also, apparently, a whore, sleeping around first with the King of France

and then with King Henry VIII. Other people have no idea who
she was at all.

Mary Boleyn was the sister of Anne Boleyn, who would
eventually become the second wife of Henry VIII only to meet her
end by a French executioner's sword three years after her marriage.
Mary Boleyn is often overshadowed by her more famous sister, but
Mary was quite a remarkable woman herself. She travelled overseas,
spent time learning and furthering her skills and knowledge in
France, she married a well-to-do man at court – a cousin to the king
no less. She had two children, of whom there continues to this day
great speculation whether they were the children of Henry VIII.
She tasted the rewards of success and faced the scant world of being
cast off. She defied her father, even her sister the queen, and married
for love. She survived her family's tragic fall from grace and lived
on with a man she loved deeply and with her whole heart. Her life
ended with no record or pomp, but she left this world quietly with
little recognition for the life she had led. Mary Boleyn was quite a
remarkable woman because she defied the social rules of the time
and followed the greatest feeling and passion a person can have –
love. Simple, uncomplicated, overwhelming love.

Many so-called facts about Mary Boleyn contradict themselves.
Authors take one stance on Mary's life while others write something
else entirely. There is confusion about whether Mary was mistress
to the French king, disagreement whether she was older or younger
than Anne, and even on the date of her death. With such differences
it becomes hard to sort fact from fiction. What was needed was a
simple source that gave all the information that is known about
Mary's life, and that is how this little book was born.

Boleyn Family Tree

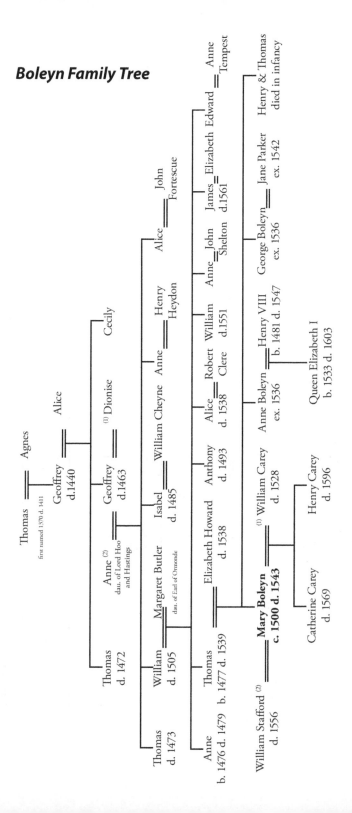

Butler Family Tree

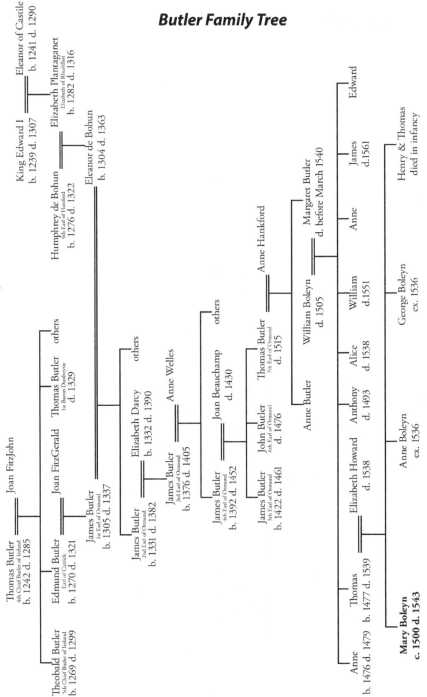

Howard Family Tree

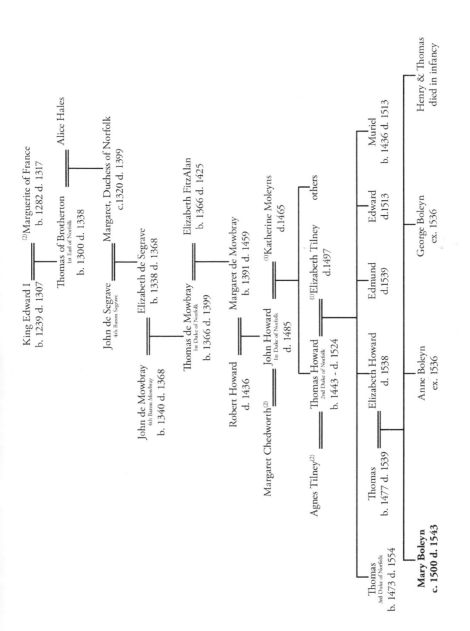

Birth

Mary Boleyn's date of birth and the location of her birth are not recorded. However, it was not uncommon for birthdates not to be recorded during the Tudor period, so the fact that Mary's date of birth has not been written down is not at all unusual.

It is generally believed that Mary Boleyn was the first child born to Elizabeth Howard and Thomas Boleyn. Thomas Boleyn was born c.1476/77 and was a prominent member of King Henry VIII's court. He was fluent in many languages including French and Latin and was well educated. He was also quick-witted and very good at sports, especially jousting, which Henry VIII also enjoyed. He used his intellect and talents to work his way up through the English court and throughout his early years there received a number of rewards. These included being knighted in 1509 and being made a Knight of the Garter in 1523. He also went on a number of diplomatic missions for Henry VIII and was ambassador for a period of time in the Low Countries and France.

Elizabeth Howard was the younger sister of Thomas Howard, 3rd Duke of Norfolk. A verse dedicated to her by the poet John Skelton relates Elizabeth to Criseyde and Irene, and as being "of womanly features, whose flourishing tender age is lusty to look on, pleasant, demure and safe", thus being very pretty.[1] Historian Kelly Hart writes that "Elizabeth, was a lady-in-waiting to Katherine of Aragon from 1509" and shared her time between the court and her home at Hever Castle.[2]

Even Thomas Boleyn's marriage to Elizabeth Howard is not recorded, but it is generally accepted that they married sometime in 1499. We do know, however, that "Elizabeth Howard's jointure was settled on her in the summer of 1501", and Eric Ives suggests that the marriage of Elizabeth and Thomas must have been relatively recent to this date.[3] In 1536, Thomas Boleyn wrote to Thomas Cromwell, right-hand man to Henry VIII, stating that "When I married I had only 50l. a year to live on for me and my wife as long as my father lived, and yet she brought me every year a child."[4] From Thomas Boleyn's statement, if we accept the couple were married in 1499, then the first child born to Thomas and Elizabeth came into the world in approximately 1500, and then four more children followed, one each year.

There has been a great deal of debate as to which daughter was eldest, Mary or Anne. The strongest evidence to suggest that it was Mary comes from a letter her grandson wrote. On 6 October 1597, George Carey, 2nd Baron Hunsdon, wrote to Thomas Cecil, Lord Burghley. He wrote that he believed he was entitled to the earldom of Ormond, which had belonged to his great-grandfather Thomas Boleyn. He stated that as the grandchild of the eldest daughter, and sole heir of Thomas Boleyn, he had a right to the title. In this

1   Norton 2013, p. 154

2   Hart 2009, p. 52

3   Ives 2009, p. 17

4   L&P xi. 17

letter George Carey also wrote that his father was Henry Carey, Mary Boleyn's son, asserting that he had a right to the earldom of Ormond.

This was a bold letter for George Carey to write. His second cousin was Queen Elizabeth I, daughter of Anne Boleyn, sister to Mary. If Anne Boleyn had been the eldest daughter then it would have been Elizabeth I who would have been entitled to the earldom of Ormond. Therefore, it can be strongly suggested that George Carey would have had to have been more than certain his grandmother was the eldest daughter of Thomas Boleyn as he was claiming the right to the title of Ormond over his second cousin the queen.

It could also be suggested that because Mary Boleyn's marriage was arranged first she would have had to have been the eldest daughter, as daughters often had their marriages arranged for them in order of age, with older daughters in the family having precedent over younger daughters.

Also, when Anne Boleyn was created Marquis of Pembroke by Henry VIII, the letters patent giving her this title referred to her as "Anne Rocheford, one of the daughters and heirs of Thomas earl of Wiltshire and Ormond, keeper of the Privy Seal."[5]. If Anne Boleyn had been the eldest daughter, would the papers not state this, especially as an older child would have precedence over a younger? Instead the letters patent simply state that she was one of the daughters of Thomas Boleyn.

In addition to this, William Camden's manuscript *Annales rerum Anglicarum et Hibernicarum regnante Elizabetha* (Annals of the Affairs of England and Ireland During the Reign of Elizabeth), published in 1615, states that Anne Boleyn was "begotten by Thomas Boleyn among other children".[6] Once again, if Anne had

---

5   L&P v. 1370

6   Quoted in Weir 2011, p. 13

been the eldest child it can be argued that Camden would have stated that.

Yet there is a small amount of evidence that contradicts the theory that Mary was the eldest daughter born to Thomas Boleyn and Elizabeth Howard. John Weever in his book *Ancient Funeral Monuments, of Great-Britain, Ireland and the islands adjacent*, published in 1767, states that within the choir of the Chapel of St Peter ad Vincula "lieth buried the body of Anne Bollein, marchioness of Pembroke, eldest daughter and coheiress of Thomas Bollein".[7] Although where Weever gathered this information from is unclear.

John Smyth in his book *The Berkeley manuscripts. The lives of the Berkeleys, lords of the honour, castle and manor of Berkeley, in the county of Gloucester, from 1066 to 1618*, published in 1883, writes that William Carey "maryed Mary second daughter and co-heiress of Thomas Bullein Earle of Wilt'shire and Ormond".[8] John Smyth was the personal attendant of Thomas Berkeley, whose wife was Mary Boleyn's great-granddaughter.

In addition to this, the script written upon Lady Berkeley's tombstone supports the evidence that Mary Boleyn was the second daughter. Lady Berkeley died in 1635, and she had been the granddaughter of Henry Carey, son of Mary Boleyn. The inscription upon her tombstone states that Mary Boleyn was the second daughter of Thomas Boleyn. This inscription completely contradicts what Lady Berkeley's father, Henry Carey, had written in his letter, stating that his mother was the eldest daughter of Thomas Boleyn.

To add even more confusion to the question, Ralph Brooke in his book *A catalogue and succession of the kings, princes, dukes, marquesses, earls, and viscounts of this realme of England*, published in 1622, writes that "Anne Bollen, eldest daughter and co-heyre of

---

7   Weever 1767, p285

8   Smyth 1883, p32

Thomas Bullen, Viscount Rochford, and Earle of Wiltshire; was created Marchionesse of Penbroke at Windfore Castle, on Sunday the first of September, 1532".[9] However, earlier in his book Brooke writes that "Anne, the second Wife of King Henry the eight, was second daughter of Sir Thomas Bullen, Earle of Wiltshire and Ormond".[10] Even in this one book the author contradicts himself, unsure if Anne was the eldest or second daughter.

Most likely Mary Boleyn was the eldest. Although there is evidence to suggest she was the second daughter, this comes from 1619 or later, over a century after Mary Boleyn was born. Also, there is no direct evidence from a relative of Mary stating she was the second daughter. There is the inscription upon the tombstone of Lady Berkeley, great-granddaughter of Mary Boleyn, but this inscription would not have been written by Lady Berkeley herself, but rather by someone who knew her. The strongest piece of evidence for Mary being the eldest comes from her grandson, George Carey. George Carey was born in 1547 and his father was the son of Mary and surely would have known when his mother was born. Therefore, the evidence strongly supports the claim that Mary Boleyn was the eldest daughter of Thomas Boleyn and Elizabeth Howard. If we believe that the couple were married in 1499 and that Elizabeth gave Thomas a child every year after their marriage, then it can be assumed that Mary was born in approximately 1500.

Where the name Mary came from is again uncertain. She may have been named after Mary Tudor, sister of Henry VIII, or perhaps the Virgin Mary. Maybe she was named after a family friend, or a distant relative. Unfortunately the reason behind the name is unknown.

It is generally believed that Mary was born at Blickling Hall in Norfolk. This assumption is made because Blickling was the Boleyn family home before Thomas Boleyn moved the family to

9   Brooke 1619, p. 277

10   Ibid., p39

Hever Castle in around 1505/06. Matthew Parker, who was Anne Boleyn's chaplain, "spoke of her coming from Norfolk, so perhaps she was at least born at Blickling".[11] If Anne Boleyn was born at Blickling, and it is believed she was born after Mary, then it can be assumed that Mary was also born there.

Mary's birth is shrouded in mystery. In Amy Licence's book *In Bed with the Tudors*, she gives details of what it was like for a late fifteenth century woman giving birth. She states that, if possible, a woman would have gone into confinement sometime before the birth, setting herself apart from the world and men. She would have hung covers over most of her windows and surrounded herself with religious artefacts, such as rosary beads. She may have also been surrounded by female family members and other female friends to provide comfort and support, especially during and after the labour. If possible a midwife would have been present as no men were allowed into the room during a woman's confinement. We can imagine Elizabeth Boleyn entering her confinement, heavily pregnant with her first child. Perhaps she was anxious, nervous of the unknown, but she may have also been excited at the prospect of having a child. We do not know if Elizabeth was happy or disappointed with the birth of her first child, a daughter.

We know that Elizabeth would go on to have four more children. In 1501, she gave birth to a second daughter, the famous Anne Boleyn. Elizabeth would also have three sons, Henry, Thomas and George. Tragically, both Henry and Thomas Boleyn would die in infancy, leaving only three Boleyn siblings to grow into adulthood.

On television and in films Mary has been portrayed as having a loving and close relationship with her brother and sister when they were children, but as they grew this relationship became distant, to the point of rivalry. However, there is little basis for this because there is no evidence that gives information on Mary Boleyn's childhood.

---

11   Loades 2011, p. 16

Education

Records tell us that in 1515 Mary Boleyn was selected as a maid-of-honour to Mary Tudor, sister of Henry VIII, who travelled to France to marry King Louis XII. Yet, as with much of Mary Boleyn's life, we know absolutely nothing about the first fifteen years. We can only make educated guesses at what Mary Boleyn's childhood was like and the type of education she received.

In 1534 Mary wrote a letter to Thomas Cromwell, asking for his assistance after she and her second husband, William Stafford, were banished from court. This letter shows us that Mary could write and read English. Eric Ives, who is one of the most renowned writers about Anne Boleyn, states that Thomas Boleyn, Mary's father, "was careful to ensure that Anne had the best available education, and he was obviously also responsible for the education of her brother, George – possibly a product of Oxford and later a recognised court poet".[12] Noticeably there is no mention of Mary's

12 Ives 2009, p. 10

education but it can be argued that as she was only a year or so older than her sister, they were educated together or shared the same tutors.

In her book *Mary Boleyn: The True Story of Henry VIII's Favourite Mistress*, Josephine Wilkinson writes that Mary received an education that was suited to a young lady of her status. She would have been taught to read and write. She would have been taught important skills such as sewing, embroidery, singing and dancing, which were all essential for a young woman. We know that at New Year 1532 Mary gave the king a blackwork collar she had made herself.[13] It therefore can be proposed that she must have been quite good at sewing to make such a gift fit for a king. She would have also learned how to play the virginal and lute. Table manners were essential as well as being taught all the necessities to conform to the religious beliefs of the time. In addition to this Mary would have been taught to ride a horse as well as some archery and hunting. Mary would also have been taught to obey men, namely her father and then her husband.

It is quite possible that Mary Boleyn learnt to speak and perhaps write in French. Her father Thomas was a diplomat and considered to be one of the best speakers of French in the English court. When Mary was chosen as a maid-of-honour to Mary Tudor, a position at the future French queen's court would have been highly sought after and it can be assumed that Thomas Boleyn used his influence to gain Mary a spot, and that she was accepted because she had at least some knowledge and skills in speaking French. Certainly, having a young woman who spoke French would have been a great help to the future queen.

It has been suggested that Mary had little or no interest in intellectual pursuits and that she had no outstanding skills or qualities that would make her attractive to others. It has also been proposed that she was dull and dim-witted, and that this is why

13   L&P v. 686

Anne was chosen instead to further her education at the court of Margaret of Austria. Or maybe Thomas Boleyn simply believed that his second daughter Anne would be more likely to be accepted into Margaret's court. However, as there are no surviving records of Mary's education, or personal notes or letters from her early years, there is no way to say this for sure. Maybe she preferred to keep to herself or she had great skills in other areas, such as sewing or playing instruments or dancing, which were all fine qualities for a young woman of the times to possess. Certainly she must have had something about her to capture the attention of Henry VIII, not only to become his mistress but to continue so for several years.

We can only briefly track Mary's whereabouts from the time of her birth until she travelled with Mary Tudor to France. It has been strongly suggested that Mary was born at Blickling Hall where her parents lived in 1500. In 1505/6, after the death of his father and Thomas Boleyn came into his inheritance, he moved his family to Hever Castle in Kent. Mary's father was a member of King Henry VIII's court and records show he was often at court or on diplomatic missions overseas. It is quite unlikely that Mary would have travelled with her father, especially as a very young child.

Kelly Hart states that Elizabeth Boleyn was a lady-in-waiting to Queen Katherine of Aragon from 1509. However, Alison Weir, in her book *Mary Boleyn: The Great and Infamous Whore*, challenges this, stating that there is no evidence that Elizabeth served Queen Katherine. Therefore, we cannot be sure if Elizabeth spent time at court or if she brought her eldest daughter there at any time during Mary's younger years. It is quite possible and most likely that Mary spent the majority of the first fifteen years of her life at her family's home at Hever.

Hever Castle, Kent.
Photo © 2015 Tim Ridgway

Personality and Appearance

One of the most frustrating aspects when researching Mary Boleyn is that there is no authenticated portrait of her. As with many people of the Tudor age there is no recorded description of what she looked like, no sketch or image for us to look upon today. In trying to work out what she may have looked like we need to try and piece together the very scant evidence that surrounds her life.

Josephine Wilkinson states: "tradition has it that Mary Boleyn was the most beautiful of the Boleyn sisters. Even she, however, did not conform to the Tudor ideal of feminine beauty, which preferred pale skin, blue eyes and blonde hair. One portrait of Mary, although it is of doubtful authenticity [the Hever Castle portrait] shows her to have a rounder and softer face than that of her sister. Her complexion is creamy, her eyes brown and, although her hair is hidden beneath her gabled hood, its colour is suggested by the shade of her eyebrows, which hint at a rich auburn or a chestnut brown."[14]

---

14   Wilkinson 2010 p. 64

Mary Boleyn "Hever" Portrait
Photo © 2015 Tim Ridgway

The portrait on display in the Inner Hall at Hever Castle is commonly believed to be a portrait of Mary Boleyn painted after the Holbein style. In the portrait we can see a woman with a slightly rounded face, wide deep brown eyes, lighter coloured skin, and light brown eyebrows and perhaps matching colour hair.

Alison Weir agrees with Wilkinson that the Hever portrait is probably not an image of Mary. Weir goes on to propose that this portrait is most likely to be Frances Brandon, eldest daughter of Mary Tudor and Charles Brandon, the Duke and Duchess of Suffolk. She states that when comparing known portraits of Charles Brandon and Mary Tudor with the Hever Castle portrait many similarities can be seen, especially with the nose and chin. Weir also moves on to state that the clothing worn by the woman in the above portrait dates to approximately the 1530s, a time when Mary Boleyn was no longer King Henry VIII's mistress and had been banished from court. Roland Hui, in his article *Two New Faces: The Hornebolte Portraits of Mary and Thomas Boleyn*, also states that the gable hood in the Hever Castle portrait dates to the mid-1530s, again, a time when Mary was banished from court and therefore certainly would not have had portraits painted of her.

One of Lucas Horenbout's most famous miniatures is of a woman painted in about 1525/26. Initially the young woman in the portrait, whose age is given as twenty-five, was believed to be Anne Boleyn. Yet there is now some debate as to whether the woman in the portrait is actually Mary Boleyn. Francesco Sanuto, a Venetian diplomat described Anne as "not one of the handsomest women in the world; she is of middling stature, swarthy complexion, long neck, wide mouth, a bosom not much raised and eyes which are black and beautiful."[15]

---

15 Calendar of State Papers and Manuscripts, Venice, Vol. 4 (1527-1533), 824

Portrait Miniature, possibly Anne Boleyn
by Lucas Horenbout, England, 1525 - 1527
With permission of the Royal Ontario Museum © ROM.

In her book *The Lady in the Tower*, Alison Weir also describes Anne as being "slender and dark",[16] whereas the woman in the Horenbout portrait appears to have a much rounder face and a pale complexion, with perhaps light brown eyebrows and possibly the same coloured hair.

In another of her books, *Henry VIII: King and Court*, Weir argues that the miniature by Horenbout cannot be of Anne Boleyn because the sitter "bears little resemblance to Anne Boleyn as she appears in the National Portrait Gallery portrait", it would have been painted when Anne's "role was little more than that of the King's low-profile inamorata, which hardly qualified her to be one of the fashionable Horenbout's first sitters", and that Anne did not adopt her famous falcon badge until 1533. Also, "the bird on her badge was rising to the right with wings elevated, while this bird is displayed apparently with wings inverted."[17]

In Roland Hui's articles *A Reassessment of Queen Anne Boleyn's Portraiture* and *Two New Faces: The Hornebolte Portraits of Mary and Thomas Boleyn*, Hui also argues that the Horenbout portrait does not resemble the image of Anne Boleyn presented at the National Portrait Gallery in London. Hui states that the National Portrait Gallery portrait of Anne Boleyn shows a woman with a long face and high cheekbones whereas the lady in the Horenbout portrait has broader features and a double chin. He also states that it was recorded that the lady in the portrait was twenty-five when the portrait was painted. Mary Boleyn was twenty-five in 1525 (when the portrait was painted), therefore Mary's age would match that of the sitter almost exactly. Hui moves on to propose that as it was William Carey, who married Mary Boleyn in 1520, that introduced Horenbout to the English court, it would not have been unusual for Carey to commission a portrait of his wife from Horenbout.

---

16   Weir 2009, p. 160

17   Weir 2008, p. 264 – 265

Hui also proposes that the Horenbout miniature may have an accompanying piece, that being a miniature of Thomas Boleyn, Mary's father. Hui suggests that the two portraits may have been painted in celebration of Thomas Boleyn being created Viscount Rochford (June 1525) and also for Mary Boleyn giving birth to a healthy son, a child who may have been the illegitimate son of King Henry VIII.

Unfortunately, Horenbout did not leave a name attached to the back of the miniature but collating the evidence above - the date the miniature was painted, Mary Boleyn's age, her husband's relationship to Horenbout and the lack of resemblance to Anne Boleyn - it can be argued that his portrait is in fact of Mary and not her sister Anne.

We also cannot look at Mary's parents to give us an idea of what she may have looked like. The only likeness we have of Mary's father Thomas Boleyn is a magnificent brass upon his tomb at St Peter's Church, Hever, Kent. The brass, of course, is not coloured and gives little indication of what colour skin, hair or eyes Thomas Boleyn had. The image simply shows a man with shoulder-length hair and a well-defined jaw with large eyes and full lips. There are also no portraits or images of Elizabeth Boleyn. It has been suggested that she was very pretty, but no further descriptions of her appearance have been recorded.

Regarding her personality, it is believed that Mary had a giddy nature, was high-spirited and enjoyed all the trappings of court life. She is not thought of as being as intelligent as her sister Anne or brother George. All of this is only conjecture and is influenced by the thoughts and opinions of people writing hundreds of years after Mary Boleyn lived. We do know that during Shrovetide 1522, when Mary was still believed to be mistress to Henry VIII, there was a lavish celebration entitled the *Chateau Vert* (or the Castle of Green). In the castle eight beautiful ladies dressed in white silk were held captive. The ladies represented virtues and Mary Boleyn played the role of Kindness while her sister, Anne, ironically played Perseverance. The virtues were guarded by eight vices played by boys from the Chapel Royal. Several lords, including the king, charged the castle and rescued the ladies. Could it be a hint at the nature and personality of Mary that she was chosen to portray the role of kindness? Or was her title selected at random? It can be argued that there must have been something about Mary Boleyn, her appearance or perhaps a spark in her personality that attracted King Henry VIII to her.

Brass of Thomas Boleyn upon his tomb
at St Peter's Church, Hever, Kent.

Brass of Thomas Boleyn upon his tomb
at St Peter's Church, Hever, Kent.

France and the English Mare

In 1514 Mary travelled from Dover to France as part of Mary Tudor's entourage and was most likely present when the English princess married King Louis XII. However, Mary's time as a lady-in-waiting was to be short as after only a few months Louis XII died. After the death of the French king, Mary Tudor scandalously married Charles Brandon, Duke of Suffolk, before returning home to England. There are several trains of thought regarding Mary Boleyn's whereabouts between this time and 1520, when she was once more recorded as being in England. Some historians suggest that Mary also returned with the dowager queen to England and became a lady-in-waiting to Katherine of Aragon. While others propose that Mary, as with her sister Anne, stayed in in France to serve the new king's wife, Queen Claude.

Alison Weir proposes that Mary was not at court as a lady-in-waiting to Katherine of Aragon, nor was she retained by Mary Tudor once she returned to England. Weir suggests that Mary's father Thomas sent her to Brie-sous-Forges (nowadays known as

Fontenay-les-Briss), a house in France owned by the new king, Francis I's cupbearer. Here, while still in France, Mary could finish off her education and polish all the necessities needed to be a noble lady. There is a tradition that Anne Boleyn lived in Brie-sous-Forges for a time, but as we know that she was retained in Queen Claude's house it is quite plausible that it was in fact Mary who went to live at Brie-sous-Forges.

Amy Licence, in her book *The Six Wives and Many Mistresses of Henry VIII*, also agrees that instead of returning to England in 1515 Mary remained in France. However, she suggests that Mary remained in the household of Queen Claude.

Whether Mary stayed only a short time or several years in France, it is often written that during her time in the country Mary became mistress to King Francis I. Her sexual activities, some say, were so well-known that even the French king referred to her as 'the English Mare', and she was said to be "a great wanton and notoriously infamous."

In her book *The Other Tudors: Henry VIII's Mistresses and Bastards*, Philippa Jones states that she does not believe that Mary Boleyn was even the mistress of King Francis I. In fact, she believes that Mary only slept with three men during her life-time, those being Henry VIII, her first husband William Carey and her second husband William Stafford. When examining the evidence used to support the assumption that Mary was the mistress of Francis I, Philippa Jones's proposal certainly gains more weight.

In fact there are only two pieces of recorded evidence that refer to Mary Boleyn's sexual activities in France. The first is a letter written by Rodolfo Pio, Bishop of Faenza on 10 March 1536. In his letter he writes:

"Francis said also that they are committing more follies than ever in England, and are saying and printing all the ill they can against the Pope and the Church; that "that woman" pretended to have miscarried of a son, not being really with child, and, to keep up the deceit, would allow no one to attend on her but her sister, whom the French king knew here in France 'per una grandissima ribalda et infame sopre tutte.'[a great prostitute and infamous above all]."[18]

When looking at this letter there are some statements that need to be questioned. First how could Mary have been with her sister when Anne miscarried in 1536? Mary Boleyn was banished from court in 1534 when she dared to marry her second husband, William Stafford, without the permission of her father, her sister the queen, or the king. It would be extremely unlikely that Mary would have been banished and then returned to court and then banished again, as there is not a single mention of her during Anne Boleyn's fall and execution, which happened less than four months after Anne's miscarriage.

Secondly, it should be pointed out that Pio wrote that "that woman pretended to have miscarried of a son, not being really with child". We know for a fact that Anne Boleyn was pregnant and that on 29 January 1536 she miscarried a male foetus when she was approximately three months pregnant. Even Eustace Chapuys, the imperial ambassador at the English court, and well known for his dislike of Anne Boleyn, wrote to his master Charles V that Anne had miscarried a male foetus.

Thirdly, it should be noted that the letter was written twenty-one years after Mary Boleyn was in France. Much can happen over the course of two decades. The relationship between England and France was sketchy at the best of times and it is clear from the tone of this letter that Francis I had little opinion of the happenings in England or of Queen Anne Boleyn. With such a sour tone, who is to say that what he was boasting about Mary Boleyn was the truth? He could have simply made the statement to blacken the name of both Mary and, more so, her sister Anne. In addition to this, Bishop Rodolfo Pio was a Catholic and may have thought very

18   L&P x. 450

little, and even been quite critical, of the Boleyns who were known to be an evangelical family.

Fourthly, how can we even be sure that what Bishop Pio wrote is the exact words that King Francis I spoke? Second-hand sources always have the disadvantage of being tainted by the person's own thoughts, feelings and beliefs. It could very well be that Francis I was not even referring to having slept with Mary, he may have just meant he believed Mary to have been a whore. It depends on how one interprets the word 'knew' in the statement. Perhaps Francois was saying he had known her in a carnal way, or perhaps he was just saying that he believed, from other sources, that Mary was a whore.

The second piece of evidence to support the idea that Mary slept with King Francis I was written by Nicholas Sander in his 1585 book *Rise and Growth of the English Schism*:

> "Soon afterwards she appeared at the French court
> where she was called the English Mare, because of her
> shameless behaviour; and then the royal mule, when
> she became acquainted with the King of France."[19]

In this statement, Sander is actually referring to Mary Boleyn's younger sister Anne and not Mary. Sander was a staunch Catholic and this book was written while he was in exile during the reign of Queen Elizabeth I, when England was considered to be a Protestant nation. Queen Elizabeth was the daughter of Anne Boleyn and these words were quite obviously written in an attempt not only to discredit and blacken the name of Anne Boleyn, but also the name of Queen Elizabeth.

It should also be noted that Sander wrote:

> "Anne Boleyn was rather tall of stature, with black
> hair and an oval face of sallow complexion, as if
> troubled with jaundice. She had a projecting tooth

---

19   Sander 1585, p.25

under the upper lip, and on her right hand, six fingers. There was a large wen under her chin, and therefore to hide its ugliness, she wore a high dress covering her throat. In this she was followed by the ladies of the court, who also wore high dresses, having before been in the habit of leaving their necks and the upper portion of their persons uncovered. She was handsome to look at, with a pretty mouth."

Most certainly we can state that Anne Boleyn did not look as though she was troubled with jaundice or that she had a projecting tooth under her upper lip. We also know that she did not have six fingers on her right hand or a large swelling under her chin. It is hard to believe that King Henry VIII would have been interested for so long in a woman who matched Sander's description.

It should also be noted that Sander's description of Anne Boleyn was written forty-nine years after Anne Boleyn's execution and most certainly would have come from second-hand knowledge. Once more with the passage of time and knowledge, descriptions can change. In addition to this, as previously stated, Sander was a staunch Catholic who was extremely prejudiced against Anne Boleyn and her daughter Queen Elizabeth I. If he was writing such lies about what Anne Boleyn looked like, how can one believe anything else he had to write?

With only two pieces of very doubtful evidence, how can it be claimed that Mary Boleyn was the mistress of Francis I and that she was a great and infamous whore? In a court full of loose morals a woman would have to do something truly outrageous to be known as an infamous whore. And yet at the time, and for over two decades later, nothing, not a single word, was mentioned about Mary Boleyn's behaviour or actions at the French court. More so, if she was so well known to have jumped into the bed of Francis I, would Henry VIII still have then taken Mary to be his mistress?

And if so, why was no comment made about her actions during her time as Henry VIII's mistress?

Was Mary Boleyn the mistress of King Francis I for a period of time? Or was she able to keep her chastity and return to England as a maid? The evidence that suggests that Mary did become the mistress of Francis I is very sketchy at best. Both pieces were written by men of the Catholic faith who were trying to discredit and blacken the name of Mary's sister Anne and Anne's daughter Queen Elizabeth I. In addition to this, Rodolfo Pio, Bishop of Faenza's letter was written approximately two decades after Mary Boleyn arrived in France and Nicholas Sander's book was written seven decades after Mary's time in France by a man who was not even born when Mary was in France.

We will never know if Mary did have an affair with Francis I, but the evidence to suggest she did is flimsy at best.

Marriage,
Royal Mistress and Children

In 1520, Mary was back in England. On 4 February 1520, in the Chapel Royal at Greenwich, she married Sir William Carey, a handsome young man who became a gentleman of the privy chamber. King Henry VIII was present at the marriage and gave the couple 6s and 8d as a wedding present. William Carey was the second son of Thomas Carey and Margaret Spencer. He was distantly related to the king, as his mother was a cousin of Margaret Beaufort, Henry VIII's grandmother. He was also a favourite of the king and shared many sporting interests with him, including a love of jousting, riding and hunting.

Mary's first child, a daughter named Catherine, was not born until 1524. Both William and Mary were approximately twenty years of age at the date of their marriage, old enough for the marriage to be legally consummated, so why was it another three years before a child was conceived?

During the marriage Mary famously became the mistress of King Henry VIII. It is not known exactly when the relationship started, but certainly during the marriage to William. It is commonly thought that Mary's relationship with the king may have started during or around Shrovetide 1522. During the Shrovetide Joust in 1522, Henry VIII rode out on his horse wearing the motto *elle mon coeur a navera* (she has wounded my heart) and it has been suggested that Henry VIII was referring to Mary Boleyn, his new or soon to be mistress.

It was also during this time that Mary's husband suddenly started to receive a number of grants. Could these grants have been the king's way of keeping Mary's husband happy? Or did the young, intelligent and favoured courtier simply receive these grants from his own merits?

It is believed that Mary's relationship with Henry VIII lasted approximately three years and is thought to have ended sometime during 1525. Most probably the relationship fizzled out on its own accord when Mary was pregnant with her second child. It is hard to accurately date the relationship as Henry VIII conducted the affair with the utmost discretion, and it is likely due to this that dates and encounters were not recorded. It should also be stated that it was not a dishonour to be a mistress of the English King. In fact, Henry VIII had previously been in a relationship with Elizabeth Blount, a beautiful young woman with whom he fathered a son, Henry Fitzroy. It appears that Henry VIII was quite accepting and proud of his son as at the mere age of six he was created 1st Duke of Richmond and Somerset.

The reason proposed that both of Mary's children, or at least one, might have been fathered by Henry VIII is that during the time when Catherine and Henry were conceived Mary was the mistress of Henry VIII. It has also been suggested that Henry would not have wished to have shared Mary with her husband, keeping her to himself during the entire period of their relationship. Also there

Catherine Carey, Lady Knollys
by Steven van der Meulen
Credit: Yale Center for British Art, Paul Mellon Collection

were rumours that Henry Carey looked quite a lot like Henry VIII and that the king gave William Carey a series of grants and appointments around the time each child was born in an attempt to keep him quiet about the happenings of his wife.

It has also been proposed that because Queen Elizabeth was very close to both Catherine and Henry Carey, it must have been because they were in fact half-brother and half-sister rather than just cousins. Queen Elizabeth knighted Henry Carey and also made him Baron Hunsdon. She also visited him on his death-bed, offering him the Earldom of Wiltshire (once owned by his grandfather Thomas Boleyn). For her part, Catherine Carey was one of Queen Elizabeth's senior ladies and upon her death Elizabeth paid for a lavish funeral. In addition to this, Mary's second child may have been named after his father, the king.

On the other hand, the arguments against the two children being fathered by Henry VIII are that it is quite possible during the time Mary was the king's mistress that she may have also been sleeping with her husband. Henry VIII never acknowledged Catherine or Henry as his children, where he had acknowledged Henry Fitzroy, the son he bore with his previous mistress Bessie Blount. It is also not uncommon for children to be named after the king of the time, even if their father's name was different.

It has also been suggested that the grants given to Henry Carey could have simply been to keep him silent and happy about his wife sleeping with the king. In addition, the reason that Queen Elizabeth showed great favour and kindness to Catherine and Henry Carey was simply because they were related, specifically that they were her maternal cousins.

One question that should be raised is why Mary Boleyn did not conceive until her known relationship with Henry VIII. It is interesting to note that Mary was married for three years before her first child was conceived and then gave birth to two children in a relatively short period of time – a time in which she was the mistress of Henry VIII. Mary's relationship with Henry is strongly thought to have ended when she was pregnant with her second child, Henry Carey. After this it is assumed that Mary continued to cohabit with her husband until his tragic death from sweating sickness on 22 June 1528. Once again it is curious as to why no other child was conceived.

It could very well be that Mary Boleyn did conceive during the period of 1520 – 1522, before her affair with Henry VIII started, and then again between 1525 – 1528, after the birth of her second child and before the death of her husband. It could just be that unfortunately Mary Boleyn was not able to carry the child to term, or that if a child or children were born they did not survive long after birth. Unfortunately, there are no records or evidence to give us even a hint of information as it was not uncommon for the time for dates of birth to be unrecorded.

It is known that Elizabeth Boleyn, Mary's mother, was able to conceive and give birth at least five times. Mary Boleyn had four younger brothers and sisters, Anne, Thomas, Henry and George, although it is believed that both Thomas and Henry Boleyn died in infancy. However the fact that Mary's mother could conceive and give birth several times does not mean that Mary Boleyn could also. When we look at her sister Anne we see that she was only able to give birth to one healthy child.

Perhaps Mary knew of and practised some sort of birth control? Birth control during the Tudor period was illegal as it was strongly believed that sexual relations were for procreation and not pleasure. Contraception in the Tudor period consisted of many varied and different methods including the man withdrawing from the woman before he ejaculated, or the taking of herbs and oils such as oil of mint, oil of rue, oil of savin and honeysuckle juice. The woman could also insert various things into her vagina such as pepper, wool soaked in vinegar, or bundles of herbs that would hopefully kill the sperm. She could even insert beeswax to cover the entrance of the cervix. The man could use a type of condom made of lambskin, which was known as a 'Venus Glove'. Could it be that Mary Boleyn knew how not to fall pregnant until a time of her choosing? Because contraception was illegal during the Tudor period, Mary Boleyn would have been risking a great deal if it became public knowledge that she was using such birth control.

Perhaps William Carey had a low sperm count. If the marriage between William and Mary was consummated on their wedding night or shortly afterwards and the couple lived as man and wife for several years, maybe he was not potent enough to make his wife pregnant. Again this is just a suggestion as we know little of William and Mary's relationship and how they lived during their marriage, although it is believed that the couple resided at court when William was in service to Henry VIII.

After the death of her first husband Mary Boleyn married a man named William Stafford, a man far beneath her station in life. In 1534 she arrived back at court visibly pregnant and was promptly banished by her sister, now the Queen of England. On 19 December 1534, Eustace Chapuys, ambassador to Charles V, wrote to his master stating:

> "The Lady's sister [Mary] was also banished from Court three months ago, but it was necessary to do so, for besides that she had been found guilty of misconduct (malefice), it would not have been becoming to see her at Court enceinte. [pregnant]."[20]

What happened to this child conceived between Mary and William Stafford is unknown. There are no records or details of the child being born so it could be that Mary miscarried or that the child died in infancy. But that Mary was pregnant does point once again to the fact that she was fertile enough to conceive.

---

20   L&P vii. 1554

Unfortunately, there is no way to say who the biological father of Catherine and Henry Carey was. However, according to the law of the time both children were William Carey's as any child born within marriage was legally belonging to the husband unless argued otherwise. Since Henry VIII never suggested that Catherine or Henry were his, both children were at least legally fathered by William Carey.

Hever Castle
Photo © 2012 Tim Ridgway

Widowhood

On 22 June 1528, tragedy struck. Mary's husband William Carey became gravely ill and, during that fateful day, died. The sweating sickness had first struck England in the fifteenth century and appeared on and off with one of the worst epidemics being in 1528. The symptoms were something like influenza or pneumonia, with the patient having pains and aches all over the body, headaches, a great thirst and horrible sweating. They would experience great exhaustion and a desire to sleep, rapid pulse rate, headaches and dizziness. Many who caught the sickness were dead within twenty-four hours. Mary's sister Anne and their father Thomas Boleyn also caught it and were gravely ill. Luckily for both they made a full recovery. Unfortunately, life was not so kind to Mary or her husband.

It has been suggested that William Carey may have been buried in a mass grave with others killed by the disease. This is plausible considering the fear and worry that existed about catching the sweat during the time. From this time until 1534 it is difficult to track Mary's whereabouts.

Upon her husband's death, Mary Boleyn was not only left a widow but she also had little means of supporting herself without a husband. In addition to this, Josephine Wilkinson states that Mary's father, Thomas Boleyn, turned his back on her as she was no longer mistress to the king, and therefore not a means of advancement for the family. Perhaps had Mary once been the mistress of King Francis I of France, Thomas was ashamed of her behaviour and that is why he all but disowned her. Or maybe he was upset that she had been unable to hold the attention of the English king for longer. Maybe he was disappointed that Henry VIII did not recognise either of Mary's children as his own. Maybe he saw little prospects of an advantageous marriage for Mary now she was in her late twenties. Or maybe he simply put his efforts and attention towards his second daughter Anne, who was by now the mistress of Henry VIII. Once again this is all speculation and we do not, and perhaps may never, fully understand the reasons why Thomas Boleyn did not willingly support Mary.

The months following her husband's death must have been difficult for Mary. It would appear that she appealed to the king for assistance as Henry VIII wrote a letter to his mistress Anne Boleyn, Mary's sister. In the letter he states that:

> "As touching your sister's matter, I have caused Walter Welze to write to my Lord [Viscount Rochford] my mind therein, whereby I trust that Eve shall not have power to deceive Adam; for surely, whatsoever is said, it cannot so stand with his honour but that he must needs take her his natural daughter now in her extreme necessity."[21]

---

21   The Harleian Miscellany, Letter IX, p55.

In addition to this letter Henry VIII also granted the wardship of Mary's son Henry Carey to Anne. Although it may seem unusual for a child to be taken away from his mother, it was quite common during the Tudor period. It also meant that Mary no longer had the pressure or financial burden to provide for her son. Instead, Mary's sister, who was in a better financial state as mistress to the king, would be able to provide a suitable education and upbringing for the young Henry Carey. Anne Boleyn provided a French scholar by the name of Nicolas Bourbon to teach Henry Carey as well as other royal wards, including Henry Norris (son of Henry Norris who would be accused of treason alongside Anne in 1536), and Thomas Hervey. It is not known what happened to Catherine Carey, daughter of William and Mary. It is very probable that she stayed with her mother during the period following her father's death.

It is also not known where Mary Boleyn lived during this time. Alison Weir proposes that Mary returned to the Boleyn family home of Hever Castle. This may have been an awkward time for her if she only had the begrudging support and assistance of her father. The thoughts and feelings of Elizabeth Boleyn, Mary's mother, regarding her eldest daughter are unknown. Mary was luckily granted an annuity of £100 on 10 December 10 1528 by the king, which had previously been granted to her husband. This provided her with a financial means to support herself and her young daughter.

There are no records or letters stating Mary's feelings towards her younger sister Anne. Much has been portrayed in films and books of the rivalry between the sisters or the bitter resentment that Mary felt towards Anne when she became mistress to the king – a position Mary once held. Mary and Anne spent the first decade of their lives together, most likely educated by the same tutor(s). It is quite possible that they built up some form of relationship together, although how deep this went is unknown. When Anne became

Queen of England she took Mary as one of her ladies-in-waiting. If this was out of love or family responsibility again is not clear. It is known that Anne and her younger brother George were close. Anne's concern for her brother when they were both held within the Tower of London in May 1536 is quite evident. Yet the siblings' relationship with their older sister Mary is not clear.

During the period 1528 to 1534, Anne Boleyn went from being mistress of the English king to being created Marquis of Pembroke on 1 September 1532. In addition to this title, the appointment also gave Anne lands worth £1,000 a year. Then, on 25 January 1533, Henry VIII and Anne Boleyn married and within sixth months she was crowned Queen of England. In September of the same year Anne gave birth to a daughter who was named Elizabeth and who was, at the time, the only legitimate heir to the English throne. Alison Weir proposes that Mary may have been jealous of her younger sister having been raised so high by the king. Yet we cannot know this for certain. Mary may have been jealous or she may have simply accepted her position in life and even been happy to see her sister so happy. Certainly, to be sister to the Queen of England was an impressive position to have. And maybe, during 1533 Mary was finding her own true love.

Mary does appear briefly in November 1530 when records show that Henry VIII gave Anne £20 to retrieve a jewel from her sister. How Mary came about this jewel, or why he wanted it back is unknown.

During the New Year's celebrations of 1532 Mary is reported to have given Henry VIII a gift of a shirt with a black collar. In return Henry gave Mary a piece of gilt plate. Alison Weir suggests that having received such a fine gift Mary may have been back at court as one of her sister's attendants. Certainly, this could be possible as Anne was rising higher and higher in the king's affections and by this time was commonly lodged close to him. It would not be unusual for Anne to choose her own sister to be one of her ladies-in-waiting.

We can also place Mary in October 1532. It is known that Mary accompanied her sister Anne and King Henry VIII to France in late 1532 when they went to meet King Francis I. Records state that Mary was one of the ladies participating in a masque to entertain the French king in a banquet held on 27 October 27. In fact, during the masque Mary followed directly behind her sister Anne, giving her precedence over the other ladies in the dance.

Mary also appears again in the records during her sister's coronation on 1 June 1533. During the procession Mary rode in the third coach behind Anne with their mother Elizabeth, and she wore a dress made of seven yards of scarlet velvet. Records also show that during the coronation ceremony Mary attended her sister wearing a gown of scarlet velvet and an ermine cloak and bonnet. It is also believed that after her sister's marriage to the king, Mary continued to be a lady-in-waiting to Anne, now the queen consort.

During late 1533 or early 1534 records tell us that Mary Boleyn married and when she returned to court in 1534 she was to cause quite a scandal. Upon her return to court Mary informed the queen that she had married and, in addition to this, she was also pregnant. With her marriage Mary had done the unthinkable, she had taken a husband without the knowledge or consent of her family. Not only this, but the man she had chosen was far beneath her family's status. The man she had chosen was William Stafford, a soldier in the garrison at Calais and a gentlemen usher to King Henry VIII. Stafford was also distantly related to Edward Stafford, 3rd Duke of Buckingham, who had been beheaded for treason in 1521.

To add to the mystery, there is little known about William Stafford's early life. He is believed to have been born in approximately 1512, making him about twelve years younger than her. He was reported to have been from Grafton but was most likely born in the village of Cottered. Having an older brother meant that William was not in line to inherit any property or money following his father's death. In fact, he may have had very little to show for his name besides his position as a soldier and a gentlemen usher to the king. He may have been fit and strong, and one can assume he had enough good looks to attract the attention of Mary Boleyn.

In 1527 it was reported that William was hired to search various barns and stacks in Berkshire looking for hidden corn stocks. Then, in April 1529, William and a friend, Richard Andrews, were reported to have purchased the lands and marriage wardship of William Somer. In November of the same year, Henry VIII personally appointed William to the position of joint sheriff of Oxfordshire and Berkshire.

Records state that William was present at the coronation of Anne Boleyn, perhaps as an attendant during the feast, but his exact role is uncertain. It could have been there that William and Mary met, as we know that Mary was in attendance to her sister. Or perhaps it was in late 1532, when Mary travelled with her sister and the king to Calais. By this time William had become a soldier and took the opportunity to move from England to Calais. Arthur Plantagenet, Viscount Lisle, was the deputy governor of Calais and seems to have shown trust in William Stafford as the young man was sent on various missions to England. It could have been during these trips to England that they continued their relationship.

Whenever William and Mary did meet, their relationship grew to the point where they fell in love and married. Unfortunately, William Stafford had little to offer Mary and despite being around thirty-four years of age Mary's father may still have made an advantageous marriage for her. Or perhaps her sister could have organised a marriage since, as Queen of England she was now the head of the Boleyn family. In short it was not Mary's responsibility to find herself a husband, it was her family's. She had taken no regard to her sister or even the king's wishes and this caused great anger from Anne. Not only this, but now the brother-in-law to the

King of England was no more than a mere soldier. It may also be that Anne was upset as she had only recently miscarried or given birth to a stillborn child. Losing a child close to full term would have been absolutely devastating, especially if that child was a longed-for male heir. She may have been frustrated and jealous that her sister was pregnant while she had only recently lost a child. Of course, this is just speculation, but whatever the exact reason for Anne Boleyn's anger, it vented itself in Mary being banished from court.

While banished, money became very tight for Mary and her husband. Thomas Boleyn not only disowned Mary but also stopped her allowance. It may also be that the £100 annuity that Henry VIII had granted Mary upon her first husband's death was stopped. It is not known where William and Mary went after their banishment from court. Alison Weir suggests they went to William's father's home in Cottered. Certainly, Mary would not have been allowed back to her childhood home at Hever. With money becoming desperate Mary wrote to Thomas Cromwell, right-hand man of the king, asking for help:

> "Master secretary, after my poor recommendations, which is smally to be regarded of me, that I am a poor banished creature - This shall be to desire you to be good to my poor husband and to me. I am sure it is not unknown to you the high displeasure that both he and I have, both of the king's highness and the queen's grace, by reason of our marriage without their knowledge, wherein we both do yield ourselves faulty, and do acknowledge that we did not well to be so hasty nor so bold, without their knowledge. But one thing, good master secretary, consider, that he was young, and love overcame reason; and for my part I saw so much honesty in him, that I loved him as well as he did me, and was in bondage, and glad I

was to be at liberty: so that, for my part, I saw that all the world did set so little by me, and he so much, that I thought I could take no better way but to take him and to forsake all other ways, and live a poor, honest life with him. And so I do put no doubts but we should, if we might once be so happy to recover the king's gracious favour and the queen's. For well I might have had a greater man of birth and a higher, but I assure you I could never have had one that should have loved me so well, nor a more honest man; and besides that, he is both come of an ancient stock, and again as meet (if it was his grace's pleasure) to do the king service, as any young gentleman in his court.

Therefore, good master secretary, this shall be my suit to you, that, for the love that I well know you do bear to all my blood, though, for my part, I have not deserved it but smally, by reason of my vile conditions, as to put my husband to the king's grace that he may do his duty as all other gentlemen do. And, good master secretary, sue for us to the king's highness, and beseech his highness, which ever was wont to take pity, to have pity on us: and that it will please his grace of his goodness to speak to the queen's grace for us; for, so far as I can perceive, her grace is so highly displeased with us both that without the king be so good lord to us as to withdraw his rigour and sue for us we are never like to recover her grace's favour: which is too heavy to bear. And seeing there is no remedy, for God's sake help us - for we have now been a quarter of a year married, I thank God, and too late now to call that again; wherefore it is the more alms to help. But if I were at my liberty and might choose, I ensure you, master secretary, for my little time, I have tried to much honestly to be in him, that I had rather beg my bread with him than to be the greatest queen in Christendom - And I believe verily he is in the same case with me; for I believe verily he would not forsake me to be a king.

Therefore, good master secretary, seeing we are so well together and does intend to live so honest a life, though it be but poor, show part of your goodness to us as well as you do to all the world besides; for I promise you, you have the name to help all them that hath need, and amongst all your suitors I dare be bold to say that you have no matter more to be pitied than ours; and therefore, for God's sake, be good to us, for in you is all our trust.

And I beseech you, good master secretary, pray my lord my father and my lady to be so good to us, and to let me have their blessings and my husband their good will and I will never desire more of them. Also, I pray you, desire my lord Norfolk and my lord my brother to be good to us, I dare not write to them, they are so cruel against us; but if, with any pain that I could take with my life, I might win their good wills, I promise you there is no child living would venture more than I. And so I pray you to report by me, and you shall find my writing true and in all points which I may please them in I shall be ready to obey them nearest my husband, whom I am most bound to; to whom I most heartily beseech you to be good unto, which, for my sake, is a poor banished man for an honest and godly cause. And being that I have read in old books that some, for as just causes, have by kings and queens been pardoned by the suit of good folks, I trust it shall be out chance, through your good help, to come to the same; as knoweth the (Lord) God, who send you health and heart's ease. Scribbled with her ill hand, who is your poor, humble suitor, always to command,

Mary Stafford."[22]

Mary's letter shows that she was a literate woman who knew how to write and it also gives us an insight into the type of woman she was and why she decided to defy the rules and marry William Stafford. She put love above wealth, status and duty.

If Thomas Cromwell replied to Mary's letter the reply no longer exists. There are also no records of Cromwell or the king providing assistance for Mary and her husband. However, as noted earlier, it is reported that Anne sent Mary some money and a golden cup. This small action may hint at the fact that Anne was not as jealous or angry at her older sister as some may suggest. It was a small gift, but one that certainly must have had some meaning behind it.

Mary's whereabouts and actions between her banishment from court in 1534 to the fall of her sister and her brother in May 1536 are not recorded. It may be that Mary returned with her husband to Calais where he continued to be a soldier and to serve Viscount Lisle. In 1539, William was appointed as one of the members assigned to welcome Anne of Cleves, who was to become Henry VIII's fourth wife, to Calais. If Mary and William did return to Calais it may have been a place of quiet comfort for Mary, being away from her family and seeking peace in the love of her husband. Whatever happened to the child that Mary was pregnant with in 1534 is unknown and Mary was to have no more children with William Stafford.

It does seem that during this time Anne Boleyn continued to be the guardian of Mary's son Henry and provided him with a good education. Nicholas Bourbon, the boy's tutor, was a French humanist and poet. He had been granted asylum in England and was known to have evangelical beliefs. Bourbon's friends were influential men such as Thomas Cromwell, Hugh Latimer and Hans Holbein.

---

22   Howard, A Collection of Letters, p.525-527.

Religion

There are no personal letters left that hint at Mary Boleyn's religious leanings, there are no mentions of her in relation to religious documents, nor are there any mentions of any religious books she may have read. She was not known to be a patron of anyone with certain religious beliefs, nor was she outward in her religious practices. But looking at England during the time of Mary's youth, her family and her second husband, one could make some suggestions as to Mary's religious beliefs.

During the early sixteenth century under the reign of King Henry VII and then King Henry VIII, England was a Catholic country. If we assume that Mary was born in 1500 and spent the first fifteen years of her life in England before going to France as a maid-of-honour to Mary Tudor, then Mary Boleyn would have been born into and spent her early years growing up within a Catholic nation. During this time it was heresy not to believe in Catholic doctrines and to practise the Catholic faith.

During the formative years of her life Mary would have been taught all the important aspects of the Catholic faith. She would have been taught about participating in mass and also the Eucharist and transubstantiation, where the bread and wine of communion would have turned into the flesh and blood of Christ. She would have learnt about confession and the need to admit sins to a priest and repent for wrongs, as well as purgatory and the importance of praying for the souls of dead loved ones. She would have been taught about the idea of needing to do good deeds for others and the concept of taking pilgrimages in order to pray to God. It is most probable that Mary would have been baptised and she could also have participated in a confirmation, where she would have stated her belief in God and the Catholic faith. Most importantly, would have believed that the pope was the head of the Catholic church and that his position was appointed by God.

Yet despite learning and practising all of these Catholic traditions, we cannot say with complete certainty that Mary Boleyn had no evangelical leanings. It is interesting to look at Anne, Mary's sister, and her religious beliefs. There have been many accusations levelled at Anne Boleyn, not only during her life but for centuries after regarding exactly where her religious beliefs lay. Some say she was evangelical, others that she was Lutheran (her brother George apparently being more Lutheran than Luther himself.) Some even say that she was a witch working for Satan. It is believed that it was Anne who introduced Henry to the book *The Obedience of a Christian Man* by William Tyndale, which spoke of kings being appointed by God as his representatives on earth and challenged the idea that the pope had any authority over them. Anne's younger brother George is also known to have a passion for religious reform and he commissioned two texts which spoke about making the Bible accessible to the common man.

In his book *The Boleyns: The Rise and Fall of a Tudor Family*, David Loades suggests that although Anne Boleyn did have some evangelical thoughts and beliefs, she was at the core still orthodox Catholic. She did introduce her future husband Henry VIII to new ideas and thoughts about religion and where the pope fitted into religion in England, but she was also a very devout woman who attended mass daily, kept books of prayers with her and practised the traditions of the Catholic faith. Before her execution, Anne swore on the sacrament twice that she had not committed adultery or incest. Swearing on the sacrament is also a Catholic tradition and belief and it would seem that Anne held these beliefs right up until her death. Yes, she did introduce Henry VIII to some new religious ideas, she did support and assist many people with evangelical leanings, and she probably shared some of their thoughts and beliefs. But that certainly does not make Anne an evangelical fanatic or a Lutheran. It is likely that Anne Boleyn did have some true evangelical beliefs and wanted to bring some reform to the Catholic church while still remaining faithful to many Catholic beliefs and practices.

We cannot be sure if Mary shared any of her sister or brother's evangelical thoughts or ideas but their passion for reform is something to keep in mind when one moves on to look at Mary's second husband.

In 1534 Mary married William Stafford. There is little record of Mary and William during their marriage, except for a few notes about William's service and some grants they were given after the death of Mary's father Thomas Boleyn. But it is interesting to note the actions of William Stafford after Mary's death. In her biography of Mary, Alison Weir states that Stafford converted to the Protestant faith and found favour under Edward Seymour, Duke of Somerset and Lord Protector of England during the reign of the young boy King Edward VI, Henry VIII's son by Jane Seymour. During Edward VI's reign England was turned into a Protestant country and people were encouraged to practise and follow the Protestant faith. Stafford seems to have prospered during this period and was made the standard bearer of Edward VI. He was also made a gentleman pensioner and granted an annuity of £100 for his service to the late King Henry VIII. However, after this he fell into difficult times and spent some time in the Fleet prison and then accumulated vast debts. which saw him exchange his annuity for a large cash payment.

In 1553, Henry VIII's eldest daughter became Queen Mary I after the death of her half-brother Edward VI. Mary had been a staunch Catholic all her life and when she became queen she returned England to the Catholic nation it had previously been before her father's break with Rome. She reversed the new religious rules her brother had made and re-joined England with the pope. It is interesting to find that during Queen Mary I's rule, William Stafford fled to Geneva. Many Protestants found refuge in Geneva and Stafford went there with his new wife and children, his sister, a cousin and several servants. Geneva was a Lutheran city and John Calvin, who was a leader in the Lutheran movement, lived there. It would also appear that Stafford and Calvin formed a friendship as Calvin was godfather to one of Stafford's sons from his second wife. It was here in Geneva that William Stafford died in 1556.

Mary's second husband was a Protestant but when did William Stafford convert to the Protestant faith? Was it during his marriage to Mary Boleyn? Or was it after her death, during the reign of King Edward VI? Did he and Mary ever speak about their thoughts and feelings towards the Protestant faith? Both Mary's brother and sister were known to interact with evangelical texts, did Mary also? Was she, like her sister and brother, open to different views and thoughts regarding religion? Did Mary share her second husband's beliefs?

Frustratingly we simply do not know. We can strongly assume that Mary was born and raised a Catholic but when we look at the religious actions of her sister, brother and second husband, one starts to wonder if Mary also had more open thoughts regarding religious reform. As with so many other aspects of Mary's life, we can only look at the little evidence we have and try to make some educated guesses as to what her religious beliefs were.

The Tower of London
Photo © 2013 Tim Ridgway

The Fall of the Boleyns

On 19 May 1536 at approximately 9am Anne Boleyn, wearing a robe of grey damask trimmed with fur over a crimson kirtle, mounted the scaffold that had been erected within the Tower of London. She had been charged with treason, for plotting the death of King Henry VIII, adultery with Mark Smeaton, Sir Henry Norris, Sir Francis Weston and Sir William Brereton, and incest with her brother George. Anne Boleyn had been found guilty of all charges and had been sentenced to death.

Two days earlier on the morning of 17 May, five men had been led from their lodgings within the Tower to their deaths upon Tower Hill. Thomas Cromwell had sent word to Sir William Kingston, the Tower gaoler, either on the evening of the 16th or early morning on the 17th, that Mark Smeaton, Sir Henry Norris, Sir Francis Weston, Sir William Brereton and George Boleyn were to be beheaded rather than hanged, drawn and quartered. All five men had been found guilty for their involvement with Queen Anne

Boleyn. The punishment for their treason was death. The men were executed in order of rank and, therefore, George Boleyn, as Lord Rochford, was the first to have his short life ended with a harsh downward stroke of the executioner's axe.

On that same day, Anne Boleyn's marriage to Henry VIII was annulled by Archbishop Cranmer. The exact grounds for the annulment of Anne's marriage to the King are unknown and even more bizarrely the mere fact that the marriage had been annulled and thus never lawful meant she had never been married to the king and thus did not commit adultery. Interestingly, all of this was overlooked and Anne was still sent to her death. Archbishop Cranmer stated that the marriage was annulled "in consequence of certain just and lawful impediments which, it was said, were unknown at the time of the union, but had lately been confessed to the Archbishop by the lady herself."[23] It has been proposed that the marriage was annulled due to a pre-contract she had during the early 1520s with a young man named Henry Percy, Earl of Northumberland. Yet in July 1532, Percy had sworn on oath that he and Anne Boleyn had not been pre-contracted to marry. Then again, on 13 May 1536, Percy wrote to Thomas Cromwell stating:

> "I perceive by Raynold Carnaby that there is supposed a pre-contract between the Queen and me; whereupon I was not only heretofore examined upon my oath before the archbishops of Canterbury and York, but also received the blessed sacrament upon the same before the duke of Norfolk and other the King's highness' council learned in the spiritual law, assuring you, Mr. Secretary, by the said oath and blessed body, which afore I received and hereafter intend to receive, that the same may be to my damnation if ever there were any contract or promise of marriage between her and me."[24]

---

23   Wriothesley, p. 41.

24   L&P x. 764

Another possible reason that Anne and Henry's marriage was annulled could be the impediment of affinity in the first degree, due to Henry's previous sexual relationship with Anne's sister Mary. Essentially he would have been marrying his sister. Thus it would have been against canon law for Henry to marry Anne. Although the pope had granted a dispensation allowing Henry to marry anyone within this degree of affinity, a law passed by the English parliament in 1534 made any previous papal dispensations invalid if they were against the laws of God. It would seem that Henry was able to pick and choose which laws he wished to use and which to overrule.

On 18 May 1536 Eustace Chapuys wrote:

> "I have also been informed that the said archbishop of Canterbury had pronounced the marriage of the King and of his mistress to have been unlawful and nul in consequence of the King himself having had connexion with Anne's sister, and that both he and she being aware and well acquainted with such an impediment, the good faith of the parents could not possibly legitimize the daughter."[25]

Chapuys was the imperial ambassador and his letter was written only one day after Anne's marriage to the king was annulled. It is interesting to note that Chapuys wrote that it was because of Henry VIII's relationship with Mary that the marriage was annulled and made no mention of an alleged pre-contract. Also, as a result of this annulment, Anne and Henry's daughter Elizabeth was declared a bastard.

If Mary's previous relationship with the king was the reason that Anne Boleyn's marriage to Henry VIII was annulled, and it seems the most likely reason, Anne's thoughts on the matter remain unknown. If Anne spoke about her sister at all during her imprisonment, no records of her words survive.

---

25   Calendar of State Papers, Spain, Volume 5 Part 2, 1536-1538, 54.

On 19 May 1536, at approximately 9am, a French swordsman stood upon a scaffold draped in black cloth and scattered with straw. He had been paid for by Henry VIII and had travelled to England to bring about Anne's death. Once upon the scaffold, Anne Boleyn turned and 'begged leave to speak to the people, promising she would not speak a word that was not good'.[26] She then asked Kingston "not to hasten the signal for her death till she had spoken that which she had mind to say".[27] It appears that Anne was determined to give a speech before her death.

Turning back to the crowd that was staring so intently at Anne, she took a deep breath and with a voice that wavered at first but grew stronger as she continued, Anne spoke:

> "Good Christian people, I have not come here to preach a sermon; I have come here to die. For according to the law and by the law I am judged to die, and therefore I will speak nothing against it. I am come hither to accuse no man, nor to speak of that whereof I am accused and condemned to die, but I pray God save the King and send him long to reign over you, for a gentler nor a more merciful prince was there never, and to me he was ever a good, a gentle, and sovereign lord. And if any person will meddle of my cause, I require them to judge the best. And thus I take my leave of the world and of you all, and I heartily desire you all to pray for me."[28]

With one clean strike of the sword Anne's head was severed from her body and the life of one of England's most famous queen's came to a tragic and final end. As Anne's brother George had been beheaded by the axe two days previously Mary Boleyn was now the only Boleyn sibling left.

26   Weir 2009, p. 266.

27   Ibid.

28   Ridgway 2012, p. 209-210.

If Mary was in Calais during May 1536 then certainly she would have known about the tragic fall and executions of her brother and sister. Calais was still part of England during this time and a great deal of trade and travel was done between England and Calais. Certainly, as even those in France and the Holy Roman Empire knew about Anne Boleyn's execution, then Mary, living in Calais, would also have known.

There are no records of Mary trying to contact either her brother or her sister during their imprisonment within the Tower of London. And, more frustratingly, Mary's thoughts and feelings regarding their tragic deaths remain unknown. One can assume that she was upset. Certainly, to lose both a brother and a sister to trumped-up charges of treason and incest must have been distressing. Mary may also have been upset that she would never have the chance to seek forgiveness from her sister and to receive Anne's blessing regarding her marriage to Stafford. We do not even know if Mary knew that it was her previous relationship with Henry VIII that was the reason behind the annulment of her sister's marriage. And if she did know, what her thoughts and feelings regarding being drawn into her sister downfall were.

Detail of the Execution Memorial at the Tower of London
Photo © 2014 Sarah Bryson

The Last Years

After May 1536, Mary seems to have slipped into obscurity again and it is difficult to place her over the next seven years.

On 3 April 1538, Mary's mother Elizabeth Boleyn died and was buried in the Howard family chapel at St Mary's, Lambeth. Although it is not stated where Mary was at this time, one possibility is that she was in Calais with her husband. We do not know Mary's feelings about her mother's death or if she returned to England for the funeral. In fact we do not even know the type of relationship Mary and her mother had in the later years of their lives. Being banished from court, it may be that Mary and her mother were estranged. If so, it is a sad ending to the relationship between mother and daughter.

Less than a year later, on 12 March 1539, Mary's father Thomas Boleyn also died. He was buried at St Peter's Church, a small church located close to Hever Castle. Once again we have no records detailing Mary's feelings upon her father's death. Mary had now lost her brother, sister, mother and father. One can only wonder if this was a difficult time for the oldest Boleyn sibling. Certainly, Mary was free from the bondage of her family's thoughts and negative reactions to her, but on the other hand, now Mary no longer had the opportunity to seek forgiveness or at least reconnect with her family.

We can assume that Mary and her husband returned to England with Anne of Cleves, or shortly afterwards, because in January 1540 William Stafford was created a gentleman pensioner to the king. Essentially he was part of a group of guards who were assigned to guard the king and keep watch in the king's presence chamber. Certainly this was a trusted position as it was up to William and his fellow pensioners to protect the safety of the king from any who would wish to harm him. William was required to wear a special gold medallion on a chain around his neck to signify his post. He also had to provide and maintain his own weapons.

With his death Thomas Boleyn left two heirs, his granddaughter Elizabeth and his daughter Mary. As Elizabeth had been declared a bastard with the annulment of her mother's marriage to the king, her share of her grandfather's inheritance went to the Crown. Mary Boleyn would have to wait a year before she was able to inherit anything from her father's death. On 15 April1540, the king granted Mary and William the manors of "Livery of lands, viz., of the manors of Southt [sic] alias Southtboram [sic] and Henden in Henden park, and all lands in Hever and Bradsted, Kent, which belonged to the said earl."[29] Mary did not inherit Hever Castle from her father as much of his property and lands reverted to the Crown. Hever Castle would eventually be given to Anne of Cleves in July 1540. It is estimated that the total worth of Mary's inheritance at this time was about £150,000 each year. Certainly, with this annual income and William's position at court, Mary's financial situation would have been eased greatly and Mary would have been able to enjoy many more comforts in life.

---

29   L&P xv. 611 (22)

In 1541, William Stafford rose once again at court and was made an esquire of the body to the king. Also in this year, Stafford exchanged "the manor of Henden, Kent, and the park called Henden parke, lands in the parishes of Bersted, Sundrisshe, and Chedyngston, Kent, and other lands sold by him to the Crown, 5 July 33 Hen. VIII" for "the manor of Uggethorpe, Yorks., and divers tenements (specified, and tenants named) thereto belonging in Lyeth, Yorks., parcel of the late priory of Gisborne, Yorks."[30] William sold the manor of Ugthorpe to Roland Shakerly.[31]

Mary Boleyn inherited Rochford Hall in Essex, but there is some confusion as to when this actually happened. It may have been in 1540 when she inherited several other manors and property, or it may not have been until 15 May 1543 when she was formally transferred the possession of the manor. Whenever Mary did inherit Rochford Hall, it is generally assumed that she and her husband lived there until her death.

Frustratingly, the exact date of Mary's death remains unknown. Mary died on either 19th July 1543 (according to Alison Weir) or 30 July 1543 (according to Josephine Wilkinson) aged approximately forty-three. She outlived her more famous sister and brother by seven years. In her biography of Mary, Alison Weir suggests it may be a possibility that Mary was buried at St Andrew's Church at Rochford. This church had been built sometime in the late fifteenth or early sixteenth century by Mary's grandfather. However, the records of the church do not go back as far as the sixteenth century and there have been extensive renovations done over the centuries so there is no record of her burial and no tombstone or brass.

Mary's relationship with her two children in the later years of her life also remains a mystery. After the death of Anne Boleyn, the wardship of Henry Carey reverted to the Crown. The king continued to provide a suitable education for the boy and, in 1545,

---

30   L&P xvi. 1308 (7)

31   Ibid., 1308 (12)

Henry Carey was made a member of the king's household. On 21 May 1545 Henry Carey married Anne, daughter of Sir Thomas Morgan of Arkstone, Herefordshire. Catherine Carey became a lady-in-waiting to Anne of Cleves and married Sir Francis Knollys on 26 April 1540, at sixteen. Catherine's first child, a son, was born in 1541.

A record in October 1542 states that a "pardon for the alienation without licence, by fine, levied" was issued to Mary and William Stafford, and Mary's daughter Catherine and her husband Francis Knollys, "of 2 messuages, 700 acres of land, 50 acres of meadow, 60 acres of pasture, 100 acres of furze and heath, common of pasture for 1,000 sheep and 59s. 2d. rent in Fulborne."[32] So they were fined, but no charges were laid. This one document suggests that Mary was in contact with her daughter and son-in-law, enough to own several properties together. It may be that mother and daughter remained close as it is likely that, after the death of her father, William Carey, Catherine stayed with her mother. Mother and daughter may have stayed together over the next few years forming a close bond. As Henry Carey was first the ward of his aunt and then the king, it may be that he had little contact with his mother. But, once again, as with much of Mary Boleyn's life, this is purely speculation based on what little evidence remains.

It is through Mary Boleyn's children, Catherine and Henry, that the Boleyn line continued, all be it with different last names. Mary's eldest child Catherine went on to have sixteen children while Mary's son Henry and his wife Anne Morgan had ten children. While not all of these children survived infancy, the majority did. Famous descendants of Mary Boleyn include Winston Churchill, prime minister of England, Charles Darwin, Elizabeth Bowes-Lyon (the late Queen Mother) and Diana, Princess of Wales. With Mary Boleyn having so many grandchildren, and those children having children and so on, then certainly over the centuries Mary

---

Boleyn's genes have been spread far and wide across the world. It is a shame that so little is known about this woman who had so many descendants, some of whom were quite famous and contributed vastly to society.

Mary Boleyn outlived her more famous sister by seven years. She appears to have found some peace and happiness in the last years of her life, away from the drama and downfall of her family. Certainly, she lived a very interesting life, being the mistress of one, perhaps two kings. One or both of her children may have been the illegitimate child/children of Henry VIII. She defied expectations and went out on her own and married for love. She was banished from court, faced great hardship but managed to find her way back to relative financial comfort. Her new husband rose at court and her children did well under Henry VIII and Elizabeth I. However, despite all of this, Mary Boleyn died in relative obscurity in July 1543. Not even the place of her burial is known. And yet it seems almost a fitting ending for a woman whose life was lived in such mystery.

Rochford Hall
Photo © geograph.org.uk

Bibliography

Abernethy, Susan. 'The English Sweating Sickness', The Freelance History Writer, 25 August 2012. http://thefreelancehistorywriter.com/2012/08/25/the-english-sweating-sickness/.

Brooke, Ralph. *A catalogue and succession of the kings, princes, dukes, marquesses, earls, and viscounts of this realme of England.* 1619.

Calendar of State Papers and Manuscripts, Venice, Vol. 4 (1527-1533).

Calendar of State Papers, Spain, Volume 5 Part 2, 1536-1538.

Castelli, J. 'Sir William Stafford of Grafton', Tudor Place. http://www.tudorplace.com.ar/Bios/WilliamStafford1.htm.

Encyclopedia Britannica, 'William Camden', http://www.britannica.com/EBchecked/topic/90745/William-Camden.

Erickson, Carolly. *Mistress Anne.* St. Martin's Press, New York, 1984.

Fraser, Antonia. *The Six Wives of Henry VIII.* Phoenix Press, London, 1992.

Friedmann, P. *Anne Boleyn*. Amberley Publishing, Gloucestershire, 2010.

Harper Karen. *The Last Boleyn: A novel*. Three River Press, New York, 1983.

Hart, Kelly. *The Mistresses of Henry VIII*. The History Press, Gloucestershire, 2009.

Hever Castle, 'Hever Castle & Gardens', 2001, http://www.hevercastle.co.uk/.

Howard, Leonard. *A collection of letters, and state papers, from the original manuscripts of several princes and great personages in the two last centuries; with some curious and scarce tracts, and pieces of antiquity, modern letters, &c...* (Volume 2). 1753

Hui, Roland. 'A Reassessment of Queen Anne Boleyn's Portraiture', 2000, http://www.oocities.org/rolandhui_2000/ab_portraiture.htm.

Hui, Roland. 'Two New Faces: The Hornebolte Portraits of Mary and Thomas Boleyn', 2011, http://tudorfaces.blogspot.com/2011/10/two-new-faces-hornebolte-portraits-of.html.

Ives, Eric. *The Life and Death of Anne Boleyn,* Blackwell Publishing, Oxford, 2009.

Jones, Philippa. *The Other Tudors: Henry VIII's Mistresses and Bastards,* Metro Books, New York, 2009.

Letters and Papers, Foreign and Domestic, Henry VIII. Edited by J S Brewer.

Licence, Amy. *In Bed with the Tudors: The Sex lives of a dynasty from Elizabeth of York to Elizabeth I',* Amberley Publishing, Gloucestershire, 2012.

Licence, Amy. *The Six Wives & Many Mistresses of Henry VIII,* Amberley Publishing, Gloucestershire, 2014.

Loades, David. *The Boleyn's The Rise & Fall of a Tudor Dynasty,* Amberley Publishing, Gloucestershire, 2012.

Loades, David and Trow, Mei. *The Tudors for Dummies,* John Wiley & Sons, LTD, West Sussex, 2011.

Loades, David. *The Six Wives of Henry VIII,* Amberley Publishing, Gloucestershire, 2010.

Luminarium, 'Luminarium: Anthology of English Literature', online encyclopaedia by Anniina Jokinen, http://www.luminarium.org/renlit/.

Meyer, G. J. *The Tudors The Complete Story of England's Most Notorious Dynasty,* Delacorte Press, New York, 2010.

Norton, Elizabeth. *Anne Boleyn In Her Own Words & the Words of Those Who Knew Her,* Amberley Publishing, Gloucestershire, 2011.

Norton, Elizabeth. *The Boleyn Women,* Amberley Publishing, Gloucestershire, 2013.

Ridgway, Claire. '17th May 1536 – Henry VIII's Marriage to Anne Boleyn is Annulled', The Anne Boleyn Files, 2011. http://www.theanneboleynfiles.com?p=9693/

Ridgway, Claire. 'Anne Boleyn's Faith', The Anne Boleyn Files, 2010. http://www.theanneboleynfiles.com?p=4990

Ridgway, Claire. 'Elizabeth Boleyn, Mother of Anne Boleyn', The Anne Boleyn Files, 2010. http://www.theanneboleynfiles.comp=?5937

Ridgway, Claire. 'Mary Boleyn – Was She Really The Mistress of Francis I?', The Anne Boleyn Files, 2011. http://www.theanneboleynfiles.com?p=15870

Ridgway, Claire. 'Sir Thomas Boleyn, Father of Anne Boleyn', The Anne Boleyn Files, 2010. http://www.theanneboleynfiles.com?p=5968

Ridgway, Claire. 'Sweating Sickness', The Anne Boleyn Files, 2010. http://www.theanneboleynfiles.com?p=6214

Ridgway, Claire. *Sweating Sickness in a Nutshell*, MadeGlobal Publishing, 2014.

Ridgway, Claire. *The Fall of Anne Boleyn: A Countdown*, MadeGlobal Publishing, 2012.

Ridgway, Claire. 'The Pregnancies of Anne Boleyn and Catherine of Aragon', The Anne Boleyn Files, 2010. http://www.theanneboleynfiles.com?p=4132

Ridgway, Claire. 'Tudor Contraception', The Elizabeth Files, 2009. http://www.elizabethfiles.com/info/tudor-life/tudor-contraception/.

Ridgway, Claire. 'What was the Sweating Sickness', https://www.youtube.com/watch?v=qwSjvIixzP8

HISTORY "In a Nutshell" SERIES

Ridley, J. *A Brief History of The Tudor Age,* Constable & Robison Ltd., London, 2002.

Rochford Hundred Golf Club. 'Rochford Hall – A Very Ancient Clubhouse', 2011.
http://www.rochfordhundredgolfclub.co.uk/brief_history_of_rochford_hundred_golf_club/chapter_7_rochford_hall_very_ancient_club_house.

Sander, Nicholas. *The Rise and Growth of the Anglican Schism* (1585), Burns and Oates, 1877.

Smyth, J. The Berkeley manuscripts. The lives of the Berkeleys, lords of the honour, castle and manor of Berkeley, in the county of Gloucester, from 1066 to 1618, Volume II, John Bellow, Gloucester, 1883.

The Harleian miscellany: or, A collection of scarce, curious, and entertaining pamphlets and tracts, as well in manuscript as in print, London, 1774.

The Dean and Chapter of Westminster. 'Henry Carey Lord Hudson & Family', 2013.
http://www.westminster-abbey.org/our-history/people/henry-carey.

The Dean and Chapter of Westminster. 'Katherine Knollys', 2013.
http://www.westminster-abbey.org/our-history/people/katherine-knollys.

The Royal Collection. 'Lucas Horenbout (c. 1505-1544)', 2001.
http://www.royalcollection.org.uk/eGallery/maker.asp?maker=12115&display=about.

Weever, J. *Ancient Funeral Monuments, of Great-Britain, Ireland and the islands adjacent,* London, W. Tooke, 1767.

Weir, Alison. *Henry VIII King & Court,* Vintage Books, London, 2008.

Weir, Alison. *Mary Boleyn: The Mistress of Kings,* Ballantine Books, New York, 2011.

Weir, Alison. *The Children of Henry VIII,* Ballantine Books, New York, 2008.

Weir, Alison. *The Lady in the Tower: The Fall of Anne Boleyn,* Jonathan Cape, 2009.

Weir, Alison. *The Six Wives of Henry VIII,* Grove Press, New York, 1991.

Wikipedia, 'Nicholas Sander',
   http://en.wikipedia.org/wiki/Nicholas_Sanders.

Wilkinson, Josephine. *Mary Boleyn The True Story of Henry VIII's Favourite Mistress,* Amberley Publishing, Gloucestershire, 2010.

Wriothesley, Charles. *A chronicle of England during the reigns of the Tudors, from A.D. 1485 to 1559,* Camden Society, 1875.

About the Author

Sarah Bryson is a researcher, writer and educator who has a Bachelor of Early Childhood Education with Honours. She currently works with children with disabilities. She is passionate about Tudor history and has a deep interest in Mary Boleyn, Anne Boleyn, the reign of Henry VIII and the people of his court. Visiting England in 2009 furthered her passion and when she returned home she started a website, **queentohistory.com**, and a Facebook page about Tudor history. Sarah lives in Australia, enjoys reading, writing, Tudor costume enactment and wishes to return to England one day.

Sweating Sickness
in a nutshell

History
"In a Nutshell"
Series

CLAIRE RIDGWAY

In **Sweating Sickness in a Nutshell**, Claire Ridgway examines what the historical sources say about the five epidemics of the mystery disease which hit England between 1485 and 1551, and considers the symptoms, who it affected, the treatments, theories regarding its cause and why it only affected English people.

MadeGlobal Publishing

Non-Fiction History

- Jasper Tudor - **Debra Bayani**
- Illustrated Kings and Queens of England - **Claire Ridgway**
- A History of the English Monarchy - **Gareth Russell**
- The Fall of Anne Boleyn - **Claire Ridgway**
- George Boleyn: Tudor Poet, Courtier & Diplomat - **Claire Ridgway**
- The Anne Boleyn Collection - **Claire Ridgway**
- The Anne Boleyn Collection II - **Claire Ridgway**
- Sweating Sickness in an Nutshell - **Claire Ridgway**
- On This Day in Tudor History - **Claire Ridgway**
- Two Gentleman Poets at the Court of Henry VIII - **Edmond Bapst**
- A Mountain Road - **Douglas Weddell Thompson**

Historical Fiction

- Cor Rotto - **Adrienne Dillard**
- The Claimant - **Simon Anderson**
- The Truth of the Line - **Melanie V. Taylor**
- The Merry Wives of Henry VIII - **Ann Nonny**

Other Books

- Easy Alternate Day Fasting - **Beth Christian**
- 100 Under 500 Calorie Meals - **Beth Christian**
- 100 Under 200 Calorie Desserts - **Beth Christian**
- 100 Under 500 Calorie Vegetarian Meals - **Beth Christian**
- Interviews with Indie Authors - **Claire Ridgway**
- Popular - **Gareth Russell**
- The Immaculate Deception - **Gareth Russell**
- The Walls of Truth - **Melanie V. Taylor**
- Talia's Adventures - **Verity Ridgway**
- Las Aventuras de Talia (Spanish) - **Verity Ridgway**

Please Leave a Review

If you enjoyed this book, *please* leave a review at the book seller where you purchased it. There is no better way to thank the author and it really does make a huge difference! *Thank you in advance.*

Lightning Source UK Ltd.
Milton Keynes UK
UKOW06f0336100616

275948UK00013B/175/P